Hi Friends,

Welcome to Gracie's Colorful World. In many ways Gracie is just like you and me. Sometimes Gracie is silly and playful, while at other times Gracie can be very serious, especially when he is learning something new or embarking on an important mission. It can be very exciting. During those times, Gracie needs to be brave and harness his courage. I bet you can be brave, too. Gracie can, but it was not always that way. In the beginning, when Gracie was a baby, Alyssa, Dina and myself were his only family and we had to help Gracie find his courage—and he did. Gracie also helped us. Oh yes, he sure did.

I know one way that you can help Gracie right now. I happened to take a sneak peek at the pictures ahead, and I noticed that Gracie's Colorful World is missing all of it's beautiful color. I bet that you can make our world colorful once again.

When you turn this page, your adventure with Gracie begins. I hope that you use your beautiful imagination, and most of all, I hope that you have lots of fun.

Gracie's Colorful World

Written, Created and Illustrated by Ken Theissen.

Digital reproduction of Ken's illustrations by Eminencesys.

ISBN 978-0-578-90492-4

GRACIE'S COLORFUL WORLD

Crayon

Coloring Book

"Hi little birdie, you must be lost," said Dina as she scooped up the tiny little nestling in her hands. With no mommy bird in sight, Dina and our daughter Alyssa, who was six years old, brought the baby inside. Little did Dina know of the impact that she would have on the baby bird or that the baby bird would have on our family.

"Daddy, Daddy," Alyssa called out with excitement. "Please put Millie in the bedroom, quick! Wait until you see what me and mommy have found."

Millie is Alyssa's cat and as lovable as cats can be, they are a danger to wild birds, especially baby nestlings.

After securing Millie in the bedroom, I made my way to the patio to see what all the excitement was about. By the time I got there, Dina and Alyssa had already made a comfy little nest out of a shoe box and a small towel. Alyssa even added her toy song birds to the nest so the baby bird wouldn't be scared or lonely.

He had no feathers, just a tiny bit of gray fur and some pin like sticks on both sides that would soon become his wings. His eyes were mostly closed and no matter how hard he tried he had trouble standing up without falling over. When Alyssa fed him it looked like he almost swallowed her finger.

"We don't know what kind of bird he is Daddy, but his name is Gracie—that's the name I am giving him," Alyssa declared, as she carefully fed him.

As a family, we nurtured and nursed Gracie to help him become such an absolutely amazing, playful and beautiful Blue Jay.

From watching Gracie play hide-n-seek and catch with Alyssa's toy beads and insects, to chasing our dogs everywhere, Gracie was non-stop and he made us laugh and smile each day.

Soon Alyssa introduced Gracie to all of her favorite toys, including her toy insects which quickly became one of Gracie's favorites as well.

Although Alyssa and Gracie were playing, Gracie seemed to take this game even more seriously than the others. Upon spotting the insects, Gracie's entire posture began to change. As if he grew right in front of us, Gracie stretched his legs and neck as far as he could to survey the scene then quickly hopped over and stood bravely above the insect. With all of his might, Gracie forcefully pecked his growing beak against the toy over and over again. Each time he pecked the insect it bounced right back at him, as if the toy was alive.

Understanding Gracie's wild instinct, Dina wanted to make sure that he developed his foraging skills. Since there was a small hole in our patio screen, it meant that lots of mosquitoes and crawly bugs got in but they didn't get out ... at least, not fast enough to avoid Super Gracie and Dina.

While perched on Dina's hand she led Gracie toward the insects. The flies buzzed back and forth, the mosquitoes whined in and out of the plants, but they were no match for the team of Super Gracie and Dina.

It didn't take long for our dogs, Bella and Maggie, to warm up to Gracie or for Gracie to warm up to them.

Hmmm, what is Gracie playing with now, Bella wonders.

Bella and Maggie each have their own relationship with Gracie. Bella loves to play and, during this time, would often bring her favorite toys to Gracie.

Although Maggie also loves to play, there is one thing that she loves more than any other, and that is ... TREATS!

Maggie

Throughout the entire time that we spent raising Gracie we realized that we couldn't be selfish and the ultimate goal was to help Gracie become strong for his release back to the wild and the wonderful world that awaited him.

In June of 2015 that day finally arrived, and we were certain that he would thrive. Together, Alyssa, Dina and myself went to the tall oak tree where baby Gracie was found just a few weeks earlier. We let Gracie know how proud we were of him and how much we loved him. Then, amid tears and joy, Dina opened her comforting hands allowing him to go but he chose to stay.

As the days followed we repeated the process and he consistently came back ... until one day.

We didn't get much sleep that night. Instead, we sat and talked about Gracie. We laughed as we shared stories about our precious and funny little Blue Jay.

As the next morning began, the things I noticed missing most were the small things, such as Gracie's daily 6:20 AM wake up call. A hungry Blue Jay doesn't care how tired you may be, and if you don't wake up for him the calls will only become louder and louder.

We also found ourselves watching our step as we walked throughout our home, because when you have a Blue Jay who loves shoe laces around you never know where they will end up.

Later that day while Dina and Alyssa were at the pool they heard a small yet distinctive squawk. Immediately, they looked around and there, on the railing, was Gracie looking back at them. He swooped down and landed next to them, content to stay with his human family.

While Gracie was brave and chose to stay outside during the night, he would visit and play throughout the day.

Little did we know that with the windows open we would now need signs that read, "BE AWARE OF FLYING GRACIE" everywhere.

"ALYSSA, DUCK," Dina and I shouted as Gracie ZOOMED through the living room and inches from Alyssa's head. Let's just say that we got real good at ducking and Gracie became quite the acrobat.

We didn't mind it one bit ... as a matter of fact, we looked forward to it.

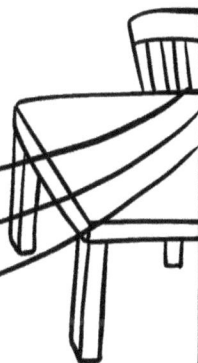

Alyssa, who was six years old at the time, was so excited to have her best friend in the whole world back.

Each day, just before nightfall, Gracie and Alyssa made their way to the front window where they would talk before Gracie flew to the tree for the night. Sometimes they stayed at the window for minutes, and other times for an hour or even more, well past Gracie's bedtime.

Storytime with Gracie is always so much fun, especially when Alyssa finds a new Horse book to share. After all, Horses are among Alyssa's favorite subjects, and Gracie seems to love them too. With a *neigh* and a *nicker* Mommy Dina reads, as we all sit around and learn all about horses.

TYPES
OF
HORSES

Although there is no place in the world that Alyssa would rather be than at the barn, when it came to raising Gracie she never wanted to leave his side.

As the summer vacation came to an end, it was the start of a new school year for Alyssa.

This wasn't the start of just any school year—it was the first grade and although we were excited, I have to admit, we were kind of nervous as well.

As we made our way to Alyssa's class we suddenly heard Gracie's distinctive Blue Jay call. "GRACIE," Alyssa called out, as she pointed toward the tree ahead. *Nah, it couldn't be*, I thought, as I kept Alyssa moving along.

Later in the day, while Alyssa was at recess with all of her teachers and classmates, Gracie suddenly flew down to the ground next to Alyssa. The kids did not know what to expect from such a friendly wild Blue Jay and the teachers were shocked ... Gracie had followed Alyssa to school!

*There is so much more about this, and other topics, in my upcoming Book.

Whew ... with Gracie following us everywhere, he can be real tough to keep up with. Sometimes he even needs some help from us to get back home, as he did when he followed Alyssa to school.

Today, it just so happens to be acorn season and Gracie can use some help finding the oak tree with the most acorns. Can you help Gracie?

It's Acorn season! Help Gracie find the Tree with the most Acorns.

YIPPEE, it's Acorn season and Gracie sure does love Acorns! Each year during Acorn season Dina, Alyssa and myself collect thousands of Acorns for Gracie to enjoy all year long. By the end of the season Gracie is perched high among a mountain full of Acorns!

"GRACIE JONES," Alyssa declares, as Gracie flies in and out, back and forth between our home to collect the Acorns and then back outside to bury them ... all while cleverly evading the neighborhood squirrels.

BEADS, CRAYONS, TOY INSECTS OR ... SNEAKERS!!!

Even before Gracie's release we learned that he absolutely loves sneakers, especially Alyssa's.

Each morning before school, Gracie makes his way inside to play with Alyssa during breakfast. Regardless of which game they play, Gracie usually finds his way to Alyssa's sneakers.

Sometimes Gracie discovers new hiding spaces for his beads inside the crevices of the sneakers, while at other times he "fiercely" pulls and pecks at them over and over again. Eventually, Alyssa's sneakers look like they've been through a Tug-Of-War with a highly-spirited gang of puppies.

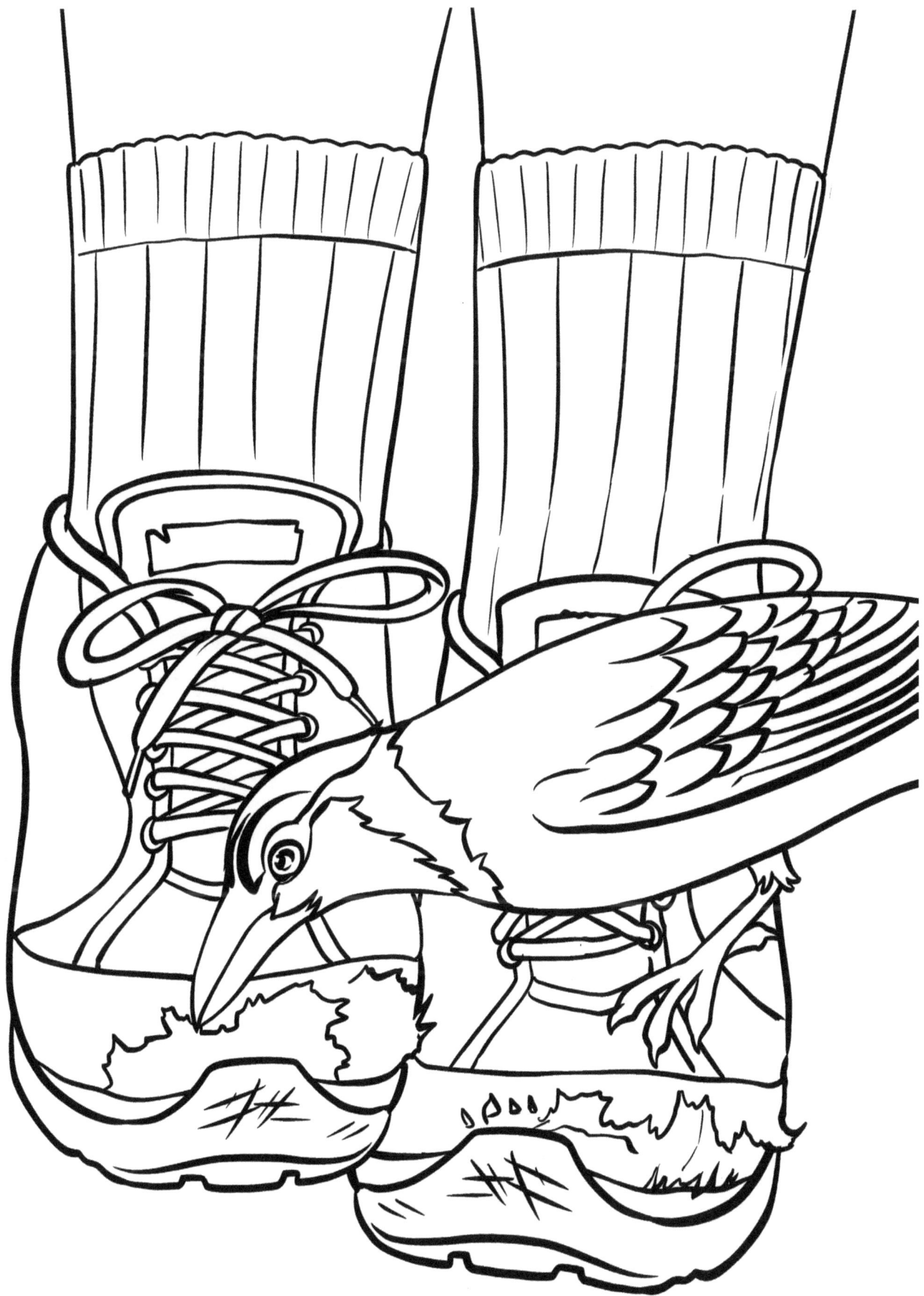

Although Alyssa's sneakers serve as a great hiding spot for Gracie's beads, he needs more hiding spots for his bigger toys, like crayons, toy insects and coins.

Oh yes, Gracie loves coins! It does not matter whether the coin is a souvenir from the Arcade or one that is used to buy our favorite treats, Gracie loves them all. And the shinier, the better!

That's where Gracie's Basket Nest comes in. He has been building and decorating his basket nest since he was just a few weeks old. Similar to an Ants home, Gracie's Basket Nest has long tunnels that were created from the folds in the small towel inside. It is within these folds that Gracie hides his favorite toys, including the coins. Often, he even flies outside with them so he can share them all with his feathery family.

Welcome to

GRACIE'S

BONK-A-WORM

Arcade Game

Of all the games that Gracie loves to play,
BONK-A-WORM is among his absolute
favorites.

Gracie is one hungry little Blue Jay and
worms are at the top of his list! Each time
his big delivery of worms comes to the door,
Gracie flies inside and right over to the
container. Once there, it is game on!

Perched high on the edge of the container,
Gracie will BONK the worms, one by one, as
they peek up from under their cardboard
hideaway.

As 2015 came to an end and a new year was beginning, Dina, my best friend and Alyssa's mommy felt a pain in her belly. Throughout the week Dina's pain and discomfort worsened, so we made an appointment with the doctor.

"Dina," the doctor said, as she held Dina's hand. "You have Ovarian Cancer. We need to prepare for surgery to remove the tumor immediately." The news was devastating.

With the same type of strength and courage seen in Gracie as he flew into the wild several months earlier, Dina was brave as the doctors brought her to the operating room.

The surgery was a success! Although there was no cancer seen elsewhere, we learned that Dina would need to undergo several months of chemotherapy. As I held her, I couldn't help but to think of the tough road ahead, while Dina, in typical fashion, expressed her positivity and spoke of never losing hope.

As a family and a team, we rallied in support of Dina, and so did Gracie! Gracie's visits throughout the day, whether long or short, really lifted everyone up and that was just what we needed ... especially Dina.

Soon the flowers began blooming, the leaves started filling the trees and Gracie seemed much busier outside during the day. Inside and out he flew, from our home for a quick visit and right back outside, all day long. On top of that, Gracie was showing all of the animals in the area just how strong and brave he was by chasing them away. From cats and squirrels, to woodpeckers, grackles and other birds, Gracie was dive bombing them all.

What in the world can he possibly be up to, I wondered, as I watched with joy and laughter. Then one day, as I followed Gracie from our home to the tree outside, I found out.

"GRACIE HAS BABIES!" I shouted, while running up the stairs to tell Dina and Alyssa. As we hugged and cheered, I thought back to the determination and love that I saw in Dina and Alyssa on the first day they rescued baby Gracie, and the incredible love for him that we all share ever since.

The discovery of Gracie's babies seemed to bring new energy to Dina, and she began spending a lot more time outside with Gracie throughout the day.

Goodbyes are not forever

That's my dad in the picture on the counter, and in August of 2015, on the same day that Gracie followed us to Alyssa's school, I realized that my dad was with us too.

Upon returning home later that day, Alyssa, Dina and myself were in the living room, still somewhat in shock over what had happened earlier, when Gracie suddenly flew inside. Instead of flying over to play with a toy or to get a treat, he flew directly to my father's picture. Although Gracie had seen the picture before, he never paid much attention to it, until now. Face-to-face with my dad, he stared, and once again I recalled the words my dad spoke to me after meeting Dina 28 years ago.

"Kenneth ... I really like Dina," he said. "She reminds me of Snow White, I can imagine all the animals coming around her." I knew right away what he meant.

In Gracie's presence, I feel my dad's spirit all around me. We had no idea what Dina was about to face just a few months down the road, but we are grateful that Gracie was there every step of the way.

With great pride and anticipation we watched Gracie's nest each day, eagerly awaiting the babies first flight. However, what we quickly discovered was something far different ... something that would take away a lot of the innocence from our life with Gracie.

"Oh no, the cat is climbing the tree to the nest," I called out to Dina, as I quickly ran down the stairs and outside. By the time I got across the street, Gracie and his mate had successfully chased the feisty feline away, but this was just the beginning.

After a challenging first nesting experience for Gracie and his mate, the babies grew to become strong fledglings and left the nest.

While inside our home one day, we all heard a faint Blue Jay call coming from outside. Together, we rushed to the patio and there they were: two absolutely adorable Blue Jay babies, perched high in the Oak Tree next to our home.

When it came time to name the babies, I looked over and watched as Gracie was chatting away while perched on Dina, then I glanced back into the tree at the babies and recalled the names that we came up with earlier: *Hope and Faith.*

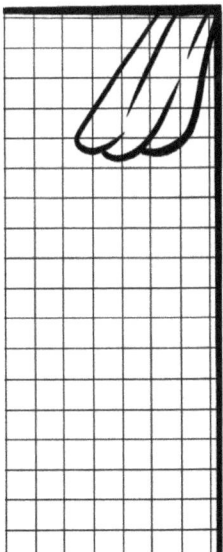

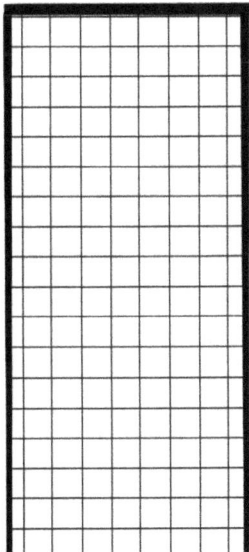

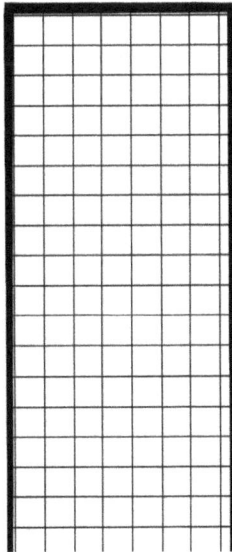

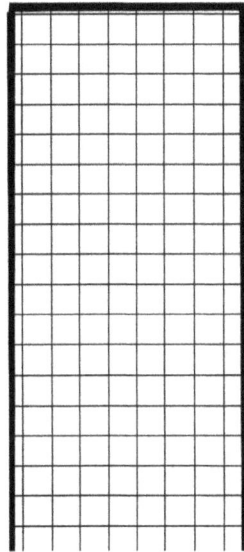

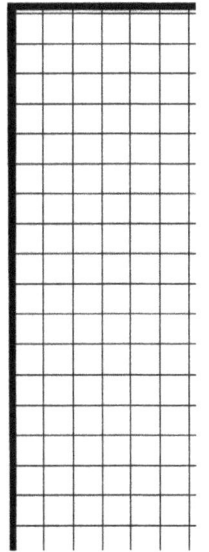

Nesting season sure does come with lots of challenges for Gracie. From building the strongest and most secure nest for his babies, to chasing away the opportunistic creatures that lurk about, Gracie is one busy Blue Jay!

However, once the babies take flight, Gracie finally has a chance to get back to one of his favorite activities in the whole entire world: BATH TIME!

Knowing how much Gracie loves his baths, we make sure that it's the "coolest" one around. With sticks and branches from nearby trees and huge plants all around it, Gracie probably feels like he's out in the forest.

When the weather in Florida becomes especially hot, I place lots of ice into the bath. Although it melts quickly, it makes the temperature perfect for Gracie. After testing the water with his beak several times, Gracie goes for it! He jumps in and shakes his little body so hard that sometimes he almost falls over. The crest on his head stands straight up, as the ice cold water sends chills throughout his body. Oh yes, it is safe to say that Gracie loves his baths.

HONK, HONK...PEEP, PEEP...QUACK, QUACK

Ah, now that's a familiar sound, and it sounds a lot like spring. This past spring, in 2021, we marked the birth of Gracie and mate's eleventh brood of babies.

Over the past six years we have experienced everything, side by side, with Gracie. And even though he has become such an intelligent, strong and brave Blue Jay, there have been times in Gracie's life that required us to spend the entire day outside with him. It is during these unique times, that Alyssa and Gracie get a chance to meet all of the neighborhood ducks.

My upcoming book, which fills in all of the details that were left out of *Gracie's Wild Adventures*, and follows our life with Gracie through today, includes all of the events surrounding the moments seen in this picture with Alyssa, Gracie and the ducks.

HAWK BUSTERS

Before Gracie's feathery family became so big, we were all that he had. In the wild, that made Gracie and his young family much more vulnerable to the never ending threats all around him.

Throughout the day we thought about what more we could do to help keep Gracie safe. When nightfall came and Gracie and his family went to sleep, I stayed awake. I couldn't help it.

Dina, who had already endured so much in her battle with Ovarian Cancer, was recovering from her third surgery; Alyssa, who was turning eight years old, had faced certain possibilities about her mommy's health that no child should ever have to think of; and Gracie's feathery family were in almost constant danger and they needed our help.

Over the years, we've used our experience to develop a strategy that keeps Gracie and his family safe from all predators...and it worked!

DRENCHED   BLASTED   BULLSEYE

Super Soakers were only part of the plan

TEAM GRACIE

HAWK BUSTERS

Yippee, it's graduation day!

Over the past six years, Gracie has experienced and overcome every obstacle imaginable to me.

I often think back to 2015, when Dina and Alyssa rescued baby Gracie. In Dina's hand, he was smaller than an egg. Baby Gracie knew nothing about the world that he would be released into just a few weeks later. Dina worked hard to teach baby Gracie the skills he needed for his successful release. In that regard, Dina could be considered Gracie's first professor; Alyssa and I would be assistant professors combined with the role of playful fellow students.

With the highest honors, Gracie has earned an education in the wild that allows him to graduate at the top of his class, and it did not come easy.

On the next page, Gracie set up a word search puzzle for us. Are you ready to try to find all of the words? I'll let you know a little secret: I asked Dina and Alyssa for help, but I still had so much fun anyway.

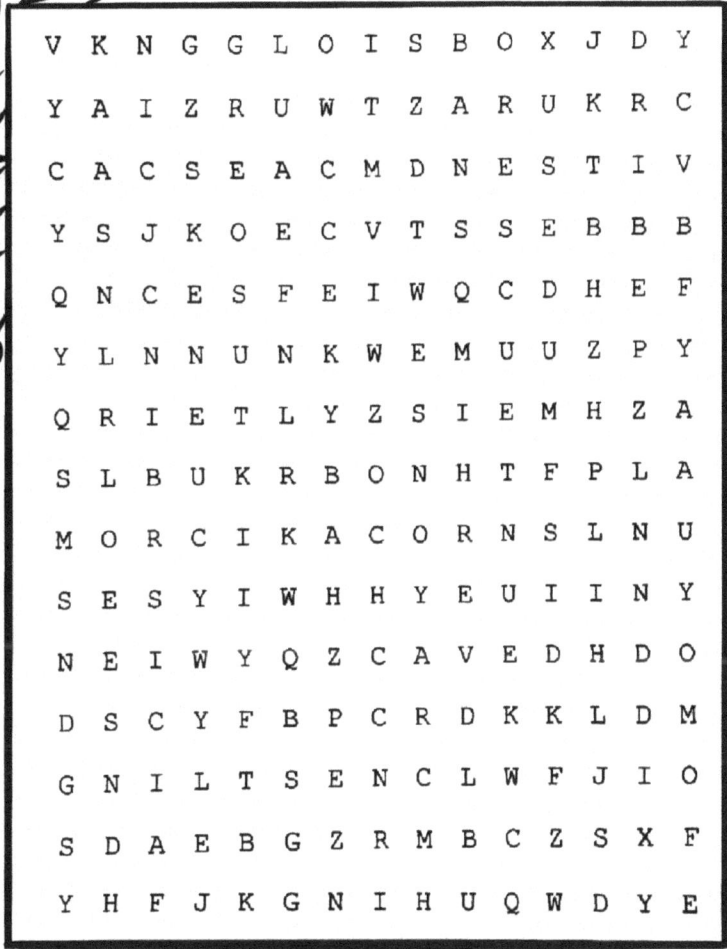

V	K	N	G	G	L	O	I	S	B	O	X	J	D	Y
Y	A	I	Z	R	U	W	T	Z	A	R	U	K	R	C
C	A	C	S	E	A	C	M	D	N	E	S	T	I	V
Y	S	J	K	O	E	C	V	T	S	S	E	B	B	B
Q	N	C	E	S	F	E	I	W	Q	C	D	H	E	F
Y	L	N	N	U	N	K	W	E	M	U	U	Z	P	Y
Q	R	I	E	T	L	Y	Z	S	I	E	M	H	Z	A
S	L	B	U	K	R	B	O	N	H	T	F	P	L	A
M	O	R	C	I	K	A	C	O	R	N	S	L	N	U
S	E	S	Y	I	W	H	H	Y	E	U	I	I	N	Y
N	E	I	W	Y	Q	Z	C	A	V	E	D	H	D	O
D	S	C	Y	F	B	P	C	R	D	K	K	L	D	M
G	N	I	L	T	S	E	N	C	L	W	F	J	I	O
S	D	A	E	B	G	Z	R	M	B	C	Z	S	X	F
Y	H	F	J	K	G	N	I	H	U	Q	W	D	Y	E

ACORNS

BEADS -

CRAYONS

INSECTS

NESTLING

ADVENTURE

BIRD

DINA

KENNY

RESCUE

ALLIE

BLUEJAY

GRACIE

NEST

"ALYSSAAA...GRACIEEE, wait for meeee!"

Something that has always been very special to me are my long bike rides with Alyssa. These bike rides took on a whole new meaning for us in the years following Dina's cancer diagnosis. Each one became an adventure, and most of them included a stop at the park or golf course to see Gracie.

Our journey began from the moment we left the garage, of which we gave a different name. We gave many things a different name. Alyssa became so immersed in this little world we had created that for the time, it was her reality.

In my upcoming book, a second edition of *Gracie's Wild Adventures* that fills in all of the details to our life with Gracie through today, I look forward to sharing this very special part of our life with you.

"Alyssa, get daddy and come out here fast," Dina called out from the patio. Even with the doors closed I could hear the calls coming from Gracie's rambunctious babies outside. By now, not only was I extremely familiar with them, but I even knew almost exactly when the new fledglings would arrive. Still, I wasn't expecting what I was about to see outside, not yet at least.

It was the summer of 2017, and Gracie and mate were in the midst of raising their fourth brood. On top of that, Gracie's first and second brood were now having babies of their own—and they were all close behind!

As I stepped onto the patio I was overcome with emotion. That happens to me a lot, but this time it was for good reason: Everywhere I looked, whether in the trees or the sky ahead of me, and even on the ground, I saw Gracie's family.

From the moment of Gracie's release, we spoke of a world for Gracie where he would be safe, surrounded by his own feathery family. That one day the trees and the skies would be filled with Gracie and his family. All of our dreams, wishes and prayers for Gracie have come true.

YIPPEE, now it's your turn to draw Gracie and he looks as cool as ever before with his favorite crayon in his beak. With crayons, beads and everything else that makes up *Gracie's Colorful World*, some may find it hard to imagine that this silly blue jay can be veeery serious when he needs to be. Oh yes, he certainly can.

Gracie's remarkable journey continues to be a huge light in our life, and a wonderful one in that. It is my wish that you, our friends and readers, can feel at least a bit of the great joy that Gracie brings to Alyssa, Dina and myself each day over the past six years, through eleven broods of babies. We are forever grateful.

All of the events written about and depicted in the illustrations throughout *Gracie's Colorful World*, and so much more, can be viewed through video and/or photographs on our Instagram page: @Gracie_the_bluejay; Facebook page: Gracie's Wild Adventures and You Tube page: Gracie The BlueJay. My first book *Gracie's Wild Adventures* is also available on Amazon and is a fun read for all ages to enjoy. The book contains 60 candid pictures showing Gracie through all of his remarkable adventures. Thank you so very much for being a part of Gracie's Colorful World.

Now it's your turn to draw Gracie. Yippee! Use the grid to help you.

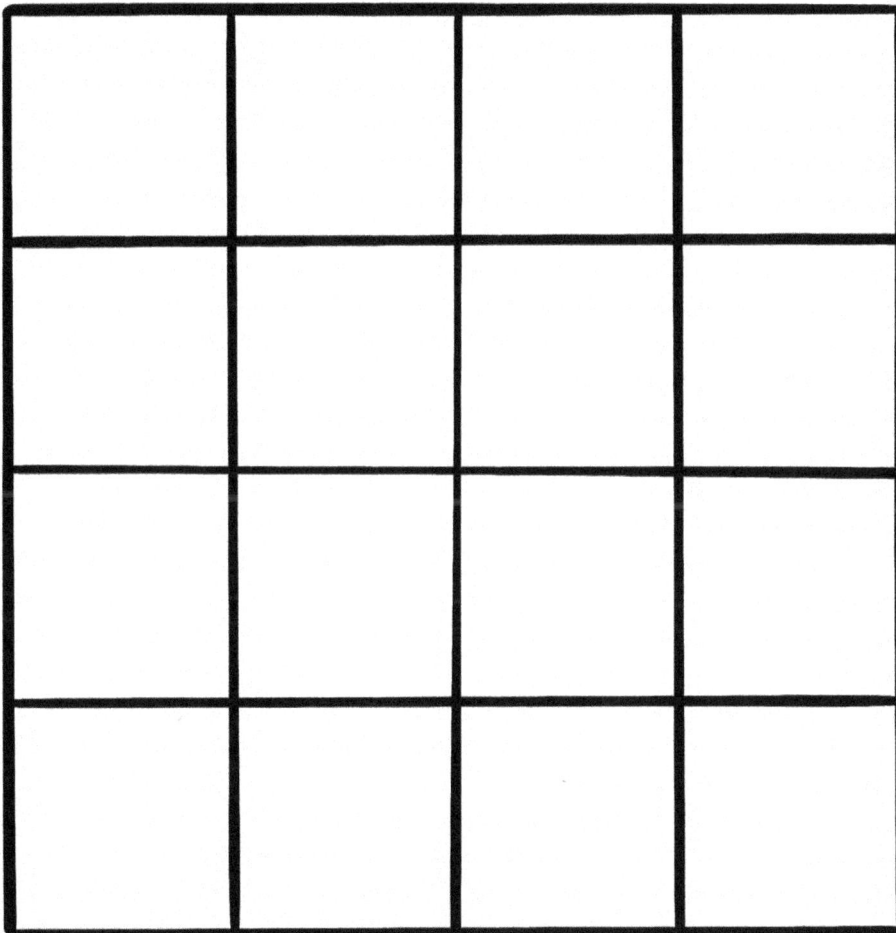

www.ingramcontent.com/pod-product-compliance
Lightning Source LLC
Chambersburg PA
CBHW051557030426
42334CB00034B/3469